Fun with Grammar

ADJECTIVES

clean

long

fancy

weak

scary

red

easy

Samantha Green

Enslow Publishing
101 W. 23rd Street
Suite 240
New York, NY 10011
USA
enslow.com

Words to Know

compare To look at things and point out what is the same and what is different.

noun A word that names a person, place, or thing.

opposite Things or words that are totally different from each other.

possessive Having to do with a word used to show whom something belongs to.

temperature How hot or cold something is.

texture How something feels on the surface.

verb A word that names an action.

Contents

Black is another adjective that can be used to describe this dog.

What Is an Adjective?

An adjective is a word that describes a person, place, or thing. It goes in front of a **noun**. In the phrase "old dog," *old* is an adjective. Dog is a noun. Adjectives help describe things around us.

Many water faucets mark hot water with red and cold water with blue.

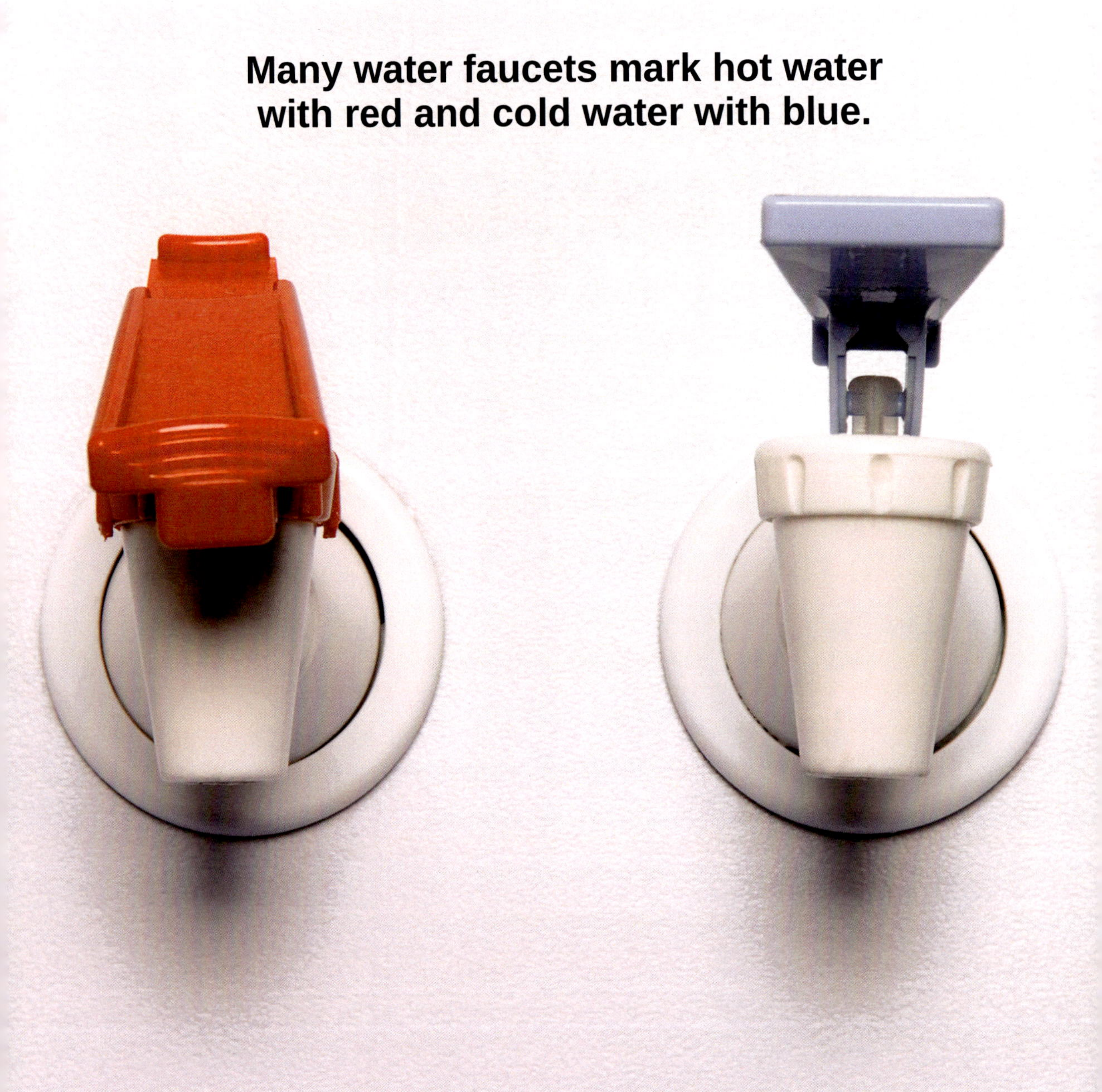

Touch Adjectives

Adjectives can describe how things feel. "The bumpy frog dances on cold ice." *Bumpy* is an adjective that describes the frog's **texture**. *Cold* is another adjective. It describes the ice's **temperature**.

FAST FACT

There are many adjectives that are opposites, like *hot* and *cold*.

This pink lollipop is *heart-shaped*.

Seeing Adjectives

We can use adjectives to talk about the way something looks. Words that describe color and size are adjectives. "That pink lollipop is so big!" *Big* is an adjective in that sentence.

Fast Fact

More than one adjective can describe a noun.

Some soups have stronger smells than others.

Smell, Sound, and Taste Adjectives

Adjectives tell us how things taste and smell. "This soup is spicy, and it smells delicious." *Spicy* and *delicious* are both adjectives. Adjectives can also describe sounds! "His voice was quiet." *Quiet* describes the way the voice sounds.

The colors used to describe these pencils are adjectives, too!

Number Adjectives

Adjectives also tell us how much of something there is. “Juan has five pencils.” *Five* tells us how many pencils Juan has.

FAST FACT

Words like *some*, *few*, and *many* are adjectives, too!

The phrase "your purple truck" has two adjectives in it: *your* and *purple*.

Possessive Adjectives

Possessive adjectives show what belongs to us. "Which truck is yours? My truck is over there." The adjective *my* tells us who owns the truck.

Fast Fact

Possessive adjectives usually answer questions that begin with which.

A *yellow* banana is good to eat.

Adjective Order

An adjective usually goes before the noun it's describing, like "yellow banana." Sometimes, adjectives go after the **verb**, like in this sentence: "Her hair is blue."

Fast Fact

When we use many adjectives, they go in a certain order: size, shape, color, noun. "That's a big, round, green ball."

The winner is *happy*, but the person who lost the game is *sad*.

Feelings Adjectives

We also use adjectives to describe how we feel and behave. "Rita is scared. I am happy." *Scared* and *happy* are both adjectives.

Fast Fact

Authors, like Roald Dahl, sometimes make up new adjectives. *Biffsquiffled* means "confused."

Elephants are the *biggest* living mammals.

Adjective Endings

We can add *-er* or *-est* to the end of adjectives to **compare** things. "The puppy is big, the horse is bigger, but the elephant is the biggest!"

Using adjectives,
we can describe
anything!

Powerful Adjectives

Adjectives are powerful! They bring our sentences to life. They help others understand what we mean, how we feel, and how we see the world.

Learn More

Books

Cleary, Brian P. *Quirky, Jerky, Extra Perky: More About Adjectives.* Minneapolis, MN: Millbrook Press, Lerner Publishing Group, 2007.

Loewen, Nancy. *The BIG Problem (and the Squirrel Who Eventually Solved It): Understanding Adjectives and Adverbs.* North Mankato, MN: Picture Window Books, Capstone Publishing, 2015.

Websites

BrainPOP: Grammar
www.brainpop.com/english/grammar
Learn about adjectives and other parts of speech with fun games, movies, and quizzes.

FunBrain: Grammar Gorillas
www.funbrain.com/games/grammar-gorillas
Help gorillas identify parts of speech in this fun game.

Index

Published in 2020 by Enslow Publishing, LLC.
101 W. 23rd Street, Suite 240, New York, NY 10011

Library of Congress Cataloging-in-Publication Data

Names: Green, Samantha, author.
Title: Adjectives / Samantha Green.
Description: New York, NY : Enslow Publishing, 2020 | Series: Fun with grammar | Includes bibliographical references and index. | Audience: Grades 1–4.
Identifiers: LCCN 2019008957 | ISBN 9781978512597 (library bound) | ISBN 9781978512573 (pbk.) | ISBN 9781978512580 (6 pack)
Subjects: LCSH: Grammar, Comparative and general—Adjective—Juvenile literature.
Classification: LCC P273 .G74 2019 | DDC 415/.5—dc23
LC record available at https://lccn.loc.gov/2019008957

Printed in the United States of America

To Our Readers: We have done our best to make sure all websites in this book were active and appropriate when we went to press. However, the author and the publisher have no control over and assume no liability for the material available on those websites or on any websites they may link to. Any comments or suggestions can be sent by email to customerservice@enslow.com.

Photo Credits: Cover, p. 1 Lopolo/Shutterstock.com; cover, p. 1 (pencil) OrangeVector/Shutterstock.com; p. 4 mythja/Shutterstock.com; p. 6 Dejan Novakov/Shutterstock.com; p. 8 © iStockphoto.com/Abby_Photos; p. 10 wong sze yuen/Shutterstock.com; p. 12 concept w/Shutterstock.com; p. 14 Shamaan/Shutterstock.com; p. 16 Ratchanee Sawasdijira/Shutterstock.com; p. 18 EvgeniiAnd/Shutterstock.com; p. 20 Inigo Cia/Moment/Getty Images; p. 22 Song_about_summer/Shutterstock.com; interior pages (notebook) Fascinadora/Shutterstock.com; interior pages (pencil) spacezerocom/Shutterstock.com